Directing
Herbert White

Other Books by James Franco

Directing
Herbert White

POEMS

James Franco

Graywolf Press

This publication is made possible, in part, by the voters of Minnesota through a Minnesota State Arts Board Operating Support grant, thanks to a legislative appropriation from the arts and cultural heritage fund, and through grants from the National Endowment for the Arts and the Wells Fargo Foundation Minnesota. Significant support has also been provided by Target, the McKnight Foundation, Amazon.com, and other generous contributions from foundations, corporations, and individuals. To these organizations and individuals we offer our heartfelt thanks.

As a work of poetry, this book is a product of the author's imagination. Places, events, incidents, and names of persons, living or dead, are used and intended to be read in an imaginative manner.

Published by Graywolf Press
250 Third Avenue North, Suite 600
Minneapolis, Minnesota 55401

www.graywolfpress.org

Published in the United States of America

ISBN 978-1-55597-673-6

2 4 6 8 9 7 5 3 1
First Graywolf Printing, 2014

Library of Congress Control Number: 2013946930

Cover design: Kyle G. Hunter

Cover art: Photo of Michael Shannon, film still, *Herbert White* (2010)

"How can I lose? In one hand I've got Marlon Brando yelling, 'Fuck you,' and in the other, Montgomery Clift asking, 'Please forgive me.'"

—James Dean to Dennis Hopper

To Frank Bidart in the left hand and Tony Hoagland in the right.
And all the other great ones between.

Contents

I.

II. The Best of the Smiths: *Side A*

III.

IV. The Best of the Smiths: *Side B*

V.

VI.

VII.

Directing
Herbert White

I.

Because

Because I played a knight,
And was on a screen,
Because I made a million dollars,
Because I was handsome,
Because I had a nice car,
A bunch of girls seemed to like me.

But I never met those girls,
I only heard about them.
The only people I saw were the ones who hated me,
And there were so many of those people,
It was easy to forget about the people who I heard
Liked me, and shit, they were all fucking fourteen-year-olds.

And I holed up in my place and read my life away,
And I watched a million movies, twice,
And I didn't understand them any better.

But because I played a knight,
Because I was handsome,

This was the life I made for myself.

Years later, I decided to look at what I had made,
And I watched myself in all the old movies, and I hated that guy I saw.

But he's the one who stayed after I died.

Film Festival

Don't be in a rush.
I have compiled a few movies,
A little film festival.
Watch and judge, you are the jury.

A little film festival in your mind.

I think you'll hate these films, because they're mine.
And I've created some sick
Things that are not nice for people to see.

First I bored everyone
And then at the end
I put in a shot of my dick
And another one with some blood.

A little film festival just for me.

All movies suck. Which ones are good?
The ones that are good, even they are no good.
You have to like no-good movies to like movies.

Now I am watching my little film festival.
And I'm my biggest fan.

It's nice when you know what you like, and I do.
I like the shape of my face and how I sit
Curled in a pose-non-pose.

James, thank you, thank you, your festival is the best.

Dear James, I don't understand your festival. You were so great in
Freaks and Geeks, *why don't you stick with that kind of stuff?*

I also killed a few people.
A little film festival just for me.

Editing

The devices make it easy now.
Smooth is what the old timers say
Is best. *The Godfather* proceeds

From scene to lapidary scene
So inevitably, who is aware
That someone arranged these shots?

•

But me, I like a bit of fast pace
Mixed with slow. I don't cut
Unless I have to. Long takes,

Give it to the actors,
Let them have their pacing
And emphasis. Viewers are too used

To polished performances from which
The editor has taken away all the messiness.
Bring in

The seams when possible: a shot that goes
Out of focus, an actor stumbling on
A line. In *Paranoid Park* there is this

Punk girl that keeps looking straight into
The camera when she speaks,
It's like she's speaking to us.

That's non-professional and only calls
Attention to the filmmakers.
So what?

Who's not aware we're watching film?
Even when the Brothers Lumière
Shot that train coming toward the camera,

And the audience got up and ran,
I'm pretty sure they knew
What was really going on.

•

It's fun to react. It may be less
Intrusive, doing long takes—
Never cutting, so

The audience is lulled into a long,
Slow meditation, a space where actor,
Director, editor, and audience

All come together and feel something.
In *Jeanne Dielman,* we sit with the prostitute
At her kitchen table,

As she pounds the meat onto the flour,
Rolls it all with an egg—two slabs—
And puts them into a bowl, and covers them,

For later, for her son.

Chateau Dreams

I picture them all, in different positions,
And the same positions,
And I, like a sculptor, would position them, and mold them.
Or like a choreographer put them through the same paces,
Again and again.

At the center of the arrangement of chalk bungalows
There is an oval pool like a blue pill,
Huddled by ferns, palms and banana trees
Tended to be wild,
Webbed by a nexus of stone walkways.

In the day,
Mermaids and hairy mermen drape the brickwork.
At night the underwater lights electrify the pool zinc blue,
The surface cradles the oven-red reflection of the neon Chateau sign
Above Sunset, above the paparazzi and miniskirts.

There is a painting of a blond sailor,
Dressed in blue and red and white,
A stoic version of myself.

For nine months in '06, while fixing my house,
I stayed in the bungalows,
First in 82, next to the little Buddha in the long fountain
Trickling.

Lindsay Lohan was about.
The Chateau was her home, the staff her servants.
She got my room key with ease,
She came in at 3 a.m.
I woke on the couch, trying not to look surprised.
I read her a short story about a neglected daughter.

Every night Lindsay looked for me.
My Russian friend Drew was always around like a wraith
—He, like the blond painting, was my doppelganger—
Writing scripts about rape and murder.
A Hollywood Dostoevsky, he gambled his money away.
We played a ton of ping pong.

•

In '82, John Belushi died from a speedball in Bungalow 3;
In '54, forty-three-year-old Nick Ray
Fucked fifteen-year-old Natalie Wood in Bungalow 2;
In 2005, Lindsay Lohan lived in room 19 for two years
Because "she didn't want to be alone."
Ambulance calls were the regular antidote to her demon nights.

Midway through my stay,
I changed to Bungalow 89.
In that room,
I read a bunch of Jacobean plays
About revenge, seduction, and lust.

In Bungalow 89
There was the sailor on the wall,
Glass eyed and pale.

The room was on the second level,
The exterior walls hugged by vines.

Every night Lindsay looked for me and I hid.

Out the window was Hollywood.

Marlon Brando

I remember when I first watched
Brando in his wife-beater
And thought I had discovered him.
And then realized three generations

Had already succumbed to his power.
He has the strength of all that America
Has to offer from its art,
He is the bull and the ballerina.

I love Stanley Kowalski and Terry Malloy
Because they are the brutes
Puppeteered by a genius.
Instead of performances

They are manifestations of a wild mind
Wrestling with its crude incarnations.
Marlon Brando is man vs. nature
And that is what we want in a man.

Like Tennessee and Blanche
We want our poetic selves
Destroyed by handsome brutes
In wife-beaters and oiled hair,

The poetry of being fucked to death.

Los Angeles Proverb

The bricks of LA were mortared with thick Indian blood,
Girls so gorgeous brown, pounded into mush and then made into stories.

Then the Spanish blood flowed in the rivers, down south, and was gone,
    except
In Sepulveda, Van Nuys, Los Feliz, Pico, San Vicente;

The streets of the City of Angels tell stories.

The movie palaces were built with the bones of ten million actresses,
And the great mansions of Bel Air and Beverly Hills and Brentwood and
    the Palisades
Are the mausoleums of naked, drugged, stupid, happy, young actors,
    all gone.

There are deals made, and they all mix and stink like the tar pit at La Brea.

LA sprawls:
Gangs, cars, palm trees, beaches, strip malls, 7-11s, smog, beaches,
Secret hideaways in the hills above Sunset,

There are four square blocks downtown, around Los Angeles Street
    and 4th
That are nothing but crack addicts.

Hollywood is an idea.
I want to get into the thix of it.

Movies won't be around forever.

II.

The Best of the Smiths

Side A

1. There Is a Light That Never Goes Out

I waited in the shadow of my stupid house.
The Mustang rolled up in the low black water,
Growling softly, then it stopped and purred.
Dark green paint like a deep flavor,
Like hard, sour-apple candy catching in my throat.

A hint of his blond swoop, the red button of his cigarette.
Smoke out the window. Sterling:
His name like a sword reflecting light in a dark room.
I'm the sword swallower.

And the grass licked my shoes.

2. Please, Please, Please

Now the picture had him in it
Up the red path
To my house
In his coal tux
Slicked like a wet cat.
I did my best in a lime-green dress.

All his gang from school:
Inside they each had some from his flask;
And Sterling smiled a toothy smile, yellow and sharp.

And then we danced.
Not to one song, but ten songs.
It was the scene where the audience came over to my side,
Because I got what I wanted.

I was in love with a cliché.

Boys his age have bodies like knives.
I was holding one by the blade.

3. Ask

I used to think about playing guitar,
Now I just listen.

With girls,
Just push and it gets there.
As soon as you hit puberty, go.
Take what comes, ugly is okay too.

With Erica, you were on someone's brother's bed;
Pothead Mormons—listen—
A flower-covered comforter, blue ground;
A drum kit in the corner of the room,
Bass drum like a bulldog and a couple of sleeping flamingo cymbals.

Gentle, but you weren't.
Love came—like viscosity filling a tube—
And you killed it with a bunch of thrusts.

Right in the middle she had to leave.
The second time she was better. Boring.

•

In the bathroom I sat naked on the floor.
Blood blooming.
—Science and fiction.
This is the rite of passage.
I am the vessel.
He is the instrument.

4. Stop Me If You Think That You've Heard This One Before

When I was in seventh grade I put kids in three categories:
Sports kids, smart kids, and social kids.

Some kids played football well and were dumb and ugly;
Some kids got great grades and their only friends were their parents;
There were others that danced among us

And made us all look like the kids we were.
They were big, daring, and sexual.
I wasn't much in any of the categories.

But in high school I met Sterling and I had *something*.

At this one party I was drunk and so was everyone else.
The sofas and chairs were floating,
And the people were shifting in their spheres,
I sat on a couch and took a ride.

Through a door to the kitchen, I saw a circus.
Plenty of colors: red and yellow and white.
There were a few ringmasters barking out things
And some lions in green letterman jackets
And this huge black seal, bonking down on this one guy, Ivan.
Bouncing him like he was a ball of air.
Until Ivan was slouched halfway to the linoleum.

One of the others hit him on the crown with a frying pan,
Like a cartoon, Ivan went all the way down and lay flat.

Sterling was on the side of it all.
Pouring foamy, piss-colored beer
Over Ivan's bloody pale face,
Laughing his electric eel grin.

His sharp dogteeth.

On the car ride home,
He drove us drunk through the dark
Like a boat
On a flat, starless sea.

5. Girlfriend in a Coma

Megan McKenna had a skinhead boyfriend,
He crashed his car into a pole.
The paramedics lifted her out of the crumpled car,
And laid her on the cement. They cut away her jeans.

Sterling and I fought all the time,
Driving around in his rotten green Mustang.
I was the sweetest sixteen,
And when we hit the other car
Darkness met me at the windshield.

My father kept Sterling from the room.
I was plastered and sutured and puffed up.

When I go to heaven,
I'll think of Sterling.
I'll think that I loved him.
I'll think that he was human.
That he was a poor little brain in a dangerous body.

III.

Acting Tips

When I played Saul
In *Pineapple Express*
I said, fuck it,
Acting should be fun.
No more twisted
Self-centered
James Dean demons.

There was one thing
That was important:
Saul should *love* Dale.
That was the secret
That made Saul
So much more
Than Harold and Kumar.

Then I played Scott Smith,
Harvey Milk's lover.
I'm still surprised
By the response
To that character.
The secret there:
Minimalism.

The film is called *Milk*,
Not *Smith*,
And that's how I played it:
A supporting lover,
Thus, as a *supporting* actor
To support Sean
Whom I love so much.

In *Howl* I played Ginsberg,
And I was all alone.
My scenes were speeches
Given to an unseen interviewer

Like Shirley Clark's
Portrait of Jason.
All I did was get down Allen's

Cadence by listening to him
Read "Howl," over and over,
All the versions
Over the course of forty years,
So many recordings.
He wrote the poem
And then the poem wrote him.

In *127 Hours* I knew
The key would be show don't tell,
Because the character just *does.*
I knew the audience
Would have an experience
Because I wouldn't be telling
Them how I feel, I'd be *feeling.*

And when the character does talk,
He does it to his little video camera;
I look right into the lens,
Ostensibly talking to my family and friends,
But I'm looking right at the audience,
So it's like a Shakespearean aside,
Without breaking the fourth wall.

And I talk about my feelings
In the most intimate way.
It's like I'm talking to the people
In the theater, as if they're all my friends,
And I'm telling them
Everything there is to know
About me.

Seventh Grade

A new school with cement all around
With wires that you can't see but feel,
And there are faces that break in at you,
And fill you with such pressure.
And you run away but the faces are always there,
Huge black ones that you never saw before.
On guys that are like grown men
That have dicks so big they could kill you.

But your dad says not to worry
Because if someone picks on you
You can handle anyone at that school, he says,
But he hasn't seen some of these guys
Because he himself wouldn't be able to handle them.
Jamal and Shaka and Ramone and Reuben,
They are different kinds of people than you have ever known.

The halls are full of these people and talk about pussy and guns
And a girl named Yvon that sucked Shaka's dick.
You try to picture it, and swallow that image whole, because it is new too,
But that world is unwieldy and can hurt you.

Instead, you have a bunch of mice at home
That had started as two, but they fucked,
Then there were twenty little pink mice in the cage.
It smelled, and you sprayed it with Right Guard.
You separated the dad from the mom, so that it wouldn't happen again
But then the mom's belly got big again with more pink things
Because one of the babies fucked her.

Think of that son,
Half her size, with barely any hair,
Riding her from behind,
Not knowing why,
But doing it because he was the strongest of the litter.

James Dean on Havenhurst

After I dropped out of UCLA
I lived on Havenhurst in Sherman Oaks,
A couple years after the earthquake rocked it
And brought the rent down.
I worked at McDonald's to pay the rent.

I stayed in a two-bedroom with two Scotts.
I slept on the couch and they had the rooms.
One Scott was from Michigan
And one was from LA.
We were all actors.

We did scenes in class:
Desire under the Elms,
The Dreamer Examines His Pillow,
American Buffalo,
True West.

One Scott went crazy,
The big one, who was an ex-Mr. Universe,
And before he went back to Grand Rapids for good,
He would lock himself in his little room
And watch four movies over and over:

East of Eden, Lust for Life,
Taxi Driver, A Place in the Sun.

A crazy boy, van Gogh,
And two murderers. It was funny
To think about the sensitive guy
That was under that Mr. Universe shell.
And scary.

The other Scott gave up too.
But he was more of a rich kid,
So, I think he did okay.

I lived there alone for at least a year.
I had so much room to stretch out,
But I didn't know what to do with it.
I put a blow-up mattress in the big bedroom
And piled my books in the dining room.

At the end of my stay
I was cast as James Dean.
I isolated myself, smoked two packs a day,
Sat on the air mattress and watched
All the Dean films, over and over:

East of Eden,
Rebel Without a Cause,
Giant.
And all the TV shows,
When he was young and goofy.

He too had dropped out of UCLA.
We were the same person.
Except, he couldn't stop being Dean,
And I could.

Fifth Grade

It was an annual field trip, for which Mrs. Yount was famous,
That and that she didn't take bullshit.
And that she had cancer, and that she was black,
And that she said often, "Shut your mouth, child," if you said something
     stupid.

On the ship trip, everyone was part of a different crew:
The rigging, or the bosun, or the fishing, or the deckhand.
We spent weeks preparing for our night on the ship,
What an amazing trip it would be.
I learned how to tie some knots,
I learned "starboard," "portside," "stern" and "bow,"
And the "capstan" and "galley" and "below deck" and all that stuff.

But what I really thought about was the coming night,
Everyone sleeping below deck, in hammocks:
If I could just sneak over to Amy Kush in the dark,
Then everything would be okay.

But her dad was Colonel Kush, a chaperone on the trip,
And what would I do if I did make it to that hammock unobserved
And lay down with her amidst all those other hammocks,
Low slung with bodies, like scrotums, no, like bells ready to clang.

And in the old days, back in 1850, what did all those sailors do,
Out on the sea for months and years?
There must be books on it.
And also many books that were never written,
Think of all the stuff that could have been written in all those books
About what happened on all those ships.

And well, shit, we were just kids,
And just docked in the harbor, for just one night.

Splash Mountain

New Orleans Square is my favorite part of Disneyland.
I spent two New Year's Eves on one of the balconies there
Watching the Mickey Mouse fireworks, sad,
And searching for something good.
Tom Sawyer Island used to be across the way
And now the Swiss Family Robinson Tree is gone.

When I was young
My dad bought us guns
From the pirate shop.
When we were older
We fingered girls in the Haunted House,
And went down Splash Mountain.

We went through Pirates of the Caribbean:
Pirates raping pigs and women, raiding
And ribaldry, men tortured, and gold taken.
Treasure and rape. And the boat floats so
Gently down the way. I want to get out and sit with the old
Man on the cabin porch.

My Place

I have a bucket on wheels and a mop, and sprays
For windows, toilets and desks.
Children write things in all places.
Fuck you Ronny. For a good time call.

I'm supposed to wipe off all the graffiti,
Especially swastikas and racial slurs.

There is a hallway outside the math building
Full of faded brown lockers
Caged in with wire fencing.
Halfway down this hall
Is a door, and inside there, my place.

There is learning happening around me all day.
But sometimes I stay late when there are no more bells
Or voices. An orange frieze above the buildings,
Soon gray and then purple when the school lights turn on.

I can sit in my room all night if I wish.
There is an industrial sink and a chair
And I have papers and notes and receipts.
And a single bare bulb on a chain, so I can see.

Each morning I wash my hands and face
But it does no good.
When kids miss the toilet, I'm the one that cleans.
When it's clogged, I put my snake in there and clear it.

There is a faculty bathroom in the office building
—Called the Tower Building—
The one-unit bathroom is for staff only,
But students sneak in there and do it.

In my place there is complete privacy.
Not many are aware of it.
I keep the door closed.

I don't even look at the girls anymore. I love movies.
I watch them on my little portable.

When the kids are gone the school is a different place.
A shadow place. I'm a shadow.

Utah

In Utah I have a driver named Jason. I drink
The sour black coffee he buys every morning

When we head to the old furniture warehouse
Called GRANIT FURNITURE. On the tan brick

Façade, above the square portals where the big
Trucks used to line their backsides and birth

New couches, the lettering angular and squat:
The G like a spaceship escape pod; the R-A-N

Missing. Inside, an exact replica of a real
Canyon in Moab, where I work daily, screaming,

Covered in corn-syrup blood and glycerin sweat.
Jason is large, like an eggplant. He's quiet.

He's just the driver and he drives. He doesn't
Listen to music or talk. Two months in, the movie moves

To Moab, four hours away, where Jason
Drives me, through sugar-dusted mountains,

Following the white box of a Fritos truck, its red
And yellow logo leading us through snow, winding

Snakewise like a hypnotist's icon. On my phone
I make videos that look like 60s home videos,

With static lines and scratches, bars rolling down
The screen: sky, snow, Jason, Fritos. On the other

Side of the mountain is desert emptiness, the sunset
Dipping and exploding on the horizon for twenty minutes.

Then in Moab, it's dark. It's Marlboro Country.

Second Grade

Mrs. D. was Mrs. Donnelly and I
Know that that means nothing to you
But to me it is a round woman
With a white bob and sharp nose
Like poultry parts.
And she was strict.

I fell in love for the first time,
Jenny Brown.
Adam Cohn loved her too.
One day we dissected fish,
And I thought of Adam when I took out the
Little guts and lay them on the tray like pebbles.

The smart kids could read whole books already.
They read *Charlotte's Web* and
The spider died.
But I couldn't read it yet.
I was still on the basics
Of sentences.

Jenny came over,
Our mothers were friends
And when the mothers left the room
We kissed.
Another time Jenny came over,
And I propped open the bathroom window,

And watched as she crouched
Girl-like on the toilet.
Jenny's father died when she was still little.
And soon after, Mrs. D. died,
Like the spider.
I'm a sensitive pig, rooting in shit.

Lindsay

Do you think I've created this?
This dragon girl, lion girl,
Hollywood hellion, terror of Sunset Boulevard,
Minor in the clubs, Chateau Demon?
Do you think this is me?

Lindsay,

Say it.
Say it, like you have ownership.
It's not *my* name anymore,
It's yours as much as mine.
So go ahead, say it.

Lind-say,

Go ahead you bookworm punk
Blogger faggot, go ahead you
Thuggish paparazzi scumbag
With your tattoos and your
Unwashed ass—

You couldn't get a girl
If your life depended on it.
Does me in your blog
Make me yours?
Do your pictures capture me?

There is someone
That I have a strange
Relationship to
That is called Lindsay,
They say she is me.

She's this strange actress
That was very
Successful as a child,
People even said
She was talented.

And then she did a sweet
Teen thing called *Mean Girls,*
And then she did a lot of other things
That got her a lot of money
And a lot of fame.

And yes, she really was a mean girl.

But that fame raped me.
And I raped it, if you know what I'm saying.
How many young things selling movies and wares
And music and tabloids fucked the kind of men I fucked?
I was 17, 18, 19.

And everyone knew it,
But they let me in their clubs,
They let me have their drugs,
They stuck their dicks in me,
And now there is not much left of me.

What do I fear?
Itsy bitsy Lindsay.
And?
One night—the year
When all was right—

Before things got bad,
I was in New York
For the premiere of a film
I did with Robert Altman
And Meryl Streep,

After the movie I took James Franco
And Meryl's two young daughters to the club
Du jour, Bungalow 8
In the Meatpacking District.
It was my place.

All my friends were there,
School friends, my mother
Looking her slutty best, bodyguards and Greeks.
We had our own table
In the corner, our own bottle.

I took two OxyContins
And things got bad.
The DJ was this bearded dude
Named Paul,
I remember requesting

Journey's "Don't Stop Believin',"
I remember sitting back down,
And I remember trying to speak up,
To talk to that cute boy
In a red gingham shirt, James.

My words rolled around
And got sticky
And didn't come out.
My friend from school
Kept talking to him,

Trying to be cute,
But she was only there because of me,
I told Barry, my bodyguard,
To take her away from our table.
And he banished her.

I took James back to the bathroom.
"You know why Amy put mirrors
All around in here?"
"Why?"
"So that you can watch yourself fuck."
He didn't fuck me, that shit.

And what was he doing there anyway?
On *my* night. My night with Meryl,
My night when everything was right,
When I got everything I wanted.
Almost.

I fucked one of the Greeks instead,
A big schnozed, big dicked,
Drunk motherfucker.
We did it in the bath.
That was the best night of my life.

IV.

The Best of the Smiths

Side B

1. This Charming Man

I'm Tom, age twelve,
On my bicycle,
I'd fly over the bike bridge to the school.
My retainer flew from my mouth,
And I let it lie on the side of the road.

My buckteeth flung themselves from my mouth,
My ears shot from my head like handles
And my nose was a blob.

Tom, will you go out tonight?

Age fifteen,
In the back of her car,
I tried it, just because—Sharon.
Because boys get with girls, right?
Even ones like Medusa.

Age sixteen,
I found I had the love life of the octopus,
Groping and grappling,
And after, slunk sideways back to my home.

I would go out tonight,
But I think I'll pass.
Just because.

Age fourteen, fifteen, sixteen, seventeen,
Erica was with Sterling
All those years,
And I was on the sideline.

    •

We all grow older.
But they won't.
Erica won't and Sterling won't.
Sterling, please.

At home,
Nineteen-ninety-three,
There are songs on my stereo that tell me big things,
And I have a religion about myself.

Kurt Cobain tells me
Where I'm going.
Sterling, there is *this* life
And there are afterlives,
And I'll see you in one of those.

2. Reel around the Fountain

In the parking lot,
In the 'stang,
After school,
Before his practice,
They kissed, hard.

Lips to lips,
Sharp teeth to sheep teeth.
A ritual.

Everyday, from then on,
I would watch
From across the lot,
One practice,

Then another.
I'd sit at the top of the bleachers,
Trying to sink into the wood.
Watching Speedos and listening to faggot jokes.

•

I have dreams of water.
I have dreams of fire.
I dream of blood.
I am all of these things.

I will never marry.

3. Hand in Glove

No other love is like this,
This special-special,
Because it's us.

When I see your chest crest above
The level of the pool,
It is Christ splashing through the blue
With a yellow ball
Here to save me.

And when I see you drive in your Mustang—
Arched behind the wheel,
Ray Bans,
Blond—
It's sexy Satan.

Graduation day,
I'll be gone.
And you,
You never knew me.

I'll keep a room
For you
In my mind.
There is a table, a chair
And a candle
That burns forever.

4. William, It Was Really Nothing

It rains.

Sterling,
It was only your whole life.
In this town,
You were king.

How could something like Erica
Capture you?
You are a force
And so am I.

Can't you see that thinking is nothing?
That school is nothing?
That family is nothing?
That girls are nothing?

I have some advice for you—
I am the center of all,
I am the core,

And all the movements you ever made
Were made to fit this poem.

5. How Soon Is Now?

I am my father's son,
Shy and vulgar,
And the heir of shit.

You say I do it all wrong.

I fill my days
With video games of love
And television shows.

Nineteen-ninety-five
Was a bad year.
You were everything—

I wiped you clean
With alcohol.

Now
I stand alone.

Something is going to happen.
Things will change.

I've erased the past,
I'm ready for the future.
For a future of *me*,
Without the need for you.

It's gonna happen
Now.

But when?

V.

31

It was birthday thirty-one,
I was in Suffolk, Virginia, directing
A short film called *Herbert White*.

We stayed at the Hilton Gardens,
The only hotel in town,
The rest are motels, rented monthly.

There are no restaurants, but plenty of strip malls,
Prefabricated houses and little swamps;
People sit in their cars in gas-station lots

And eat and smoke.
This is eating out in Suffolk.
The actor that fucks a goat in my film

Was home-schooled because his parents didn't
Want him to be subjected to drugs, guns and violence.
"And blacks," I think.

Indian River, the school is called.
Ramone is his name, a handsome, dumb-faced kid.
There were baby goats; they ran around their pen on stiff, stumpy legs.

•

I've had good and bad birthdays.
And boy do they make me think
About when I was younger,

When I had no friends and my mom drove me to school
Because I lost my license drunk-driving, and we wouldn't talk,
We would listen to *Blonde on Blonde*

Every morning, and life was like moving through something
Thick and gray that had no purpose.
And now I see that everything has had as much purpose

As I give it, or at least it can all make its way
Into my poem and become something else,
And in that way all that shit, and all those bad birthdays,

And the good ones are markers in an anniversary line—
And they carry less and less of their original pain,
And become emptier, just markers really, building blocks,

To be turned into constructions and fucked with.

They Called You Sean De Niro

On *Fast Times at Ridgemont High*
They called you Sean De Niro
Because of your dedication.
An actor as engrossed in his role
As De Niro was in LaMotta;
You were Jeff Spicoli:
Surfer, stoner, prophet.

You were smart enough to know
Not to give too much:
That ordering pizza
In class was the move
That would last.

Spicoli (in his dream) won
Surf contests, and had babes
On his arms, and was asked:
"A lot of people expected
Maybe Mark 'Cutback' Davis
Or Bob 'Jungle Death' Gerrard
Would take the honors
This year," and you said,
"Those dudes are *fags*."

And decades later,
When he introduced you
For your nomination for *Milk*,
The real De Niro, now your friend,
Said he couldn't believe you
Had been cast in all those
Straight roles, because
In *Milk* you were such
A fine homo.

When you and I kissed on Castro Street,
It was for a full minute.

Your face scratched like my father's.

Fake

There is a fake version of me
And he's the one that writes
These poems.
He has an attitude and swagger

That I don't have.
But on the page, this fake me
Is the me that speaks.
And this fake me is louder

Than the real me, and he
Is the one that everyone knows.
He's become the real me
Because everyone treats me

Like I'm the fake me.

River

Hello, James, it's River.
Where do you think I'm calling from?
Deep in hell, deep in the Florida wilderness?
Deep in the cement bowels of LA,
Beneath the neon, and the signs?

It's me, River, calling you
From the underworld.
I died at age 23,
Ten years before your age now.
James, you're the Jesus age.

You think you know me?
I tried to be something good,
Something that spoke to people,
I was pushed into acting, but I loved music,
You're in acting because you chose it.

Pick up the phone, James, it's River,
I'm calling to say it's over.
You know that moony feeling,
Like the air is gone, because there is no
More of a life? I've left just a little,

I know you want more, James,
But I left only a little.
And what time
Do we have for others
Anyway?

I've been gone for decades,
I've been forgotten.
I spent my two decades
Focused
On work and family.

You're all over the place, James.
I was a River that flowed straight
And pure; you're like a king
That orders one thing,
And then orders the opposite thing.

Hello

I am writing to you because there are so many words
That don't have form, and when I put them on paper,

They have a *little* form, but then I worry that it's not the *right* form
And then I know that my thinking is not clear.

But but but, the years go by, and decisions are made,
Like wind blowing leaves down a backlit tunnel,

Just words going round, and the form is ridiculous,
And now I think I need a little red in here, okay,

Look at the hood of her Stanford sweatshirt, the girl
I'm in love with, a fucking miracle,

A rippling blue miracle breaking on the surface of the lake,
After I've dropped my lucky penny through.

Hello down there.
Hello up there.

Hart Crane's Tomb

The guy that could fuck sailors
And throw a punch,

And whose life was so bound up
In his poetry that when he said to the Brooklyn Bridge

"A bedlamite speeds to thy parapets,
Tilting there momently, shrill shirt ballooning,"

He meant himself.
A circle on the surface of the ocean,

For a second,
And then the bottom of the sea.

Sal Mineo

I directed a film about the actor Sal Mineo.
Many people in the new generation
Might not know who he was,
Because he's been dead since '76.

My film focuses on his last day alive,
Because he lived his whole life in his last day:
He talked to his lover Sid on the phone,
About plans for the future;
He went to the gym;

He invited people, including Liz Taylor and Paul Newman
And Nick Ray to the opening of his new play,
P.S. Your Cat Is Dead;
And he went to rehearsal
With Keir Dullea of *2001* fame, and Milton Katselas,
The future guru of the Beverly Hills Playhouse.

In *P.S.* Sal played a bisexual burglar
That gets caught burgling an apartment.

Later that night, after rehearsal,
Sal was actually stabbed
By a real burglar
In front of his apartment,
On Holloway Drive.

Stabbed near his heart,
In the heart of Hollywood.

For a year they didn't capture his killer.
So the tabloids said he was killed for drugs,
Or because he was gay:
A GAY LOVE TRIANGLE KILLING.
But it was none of those things,
None of those things.

•

Don't worry, famous people;
Three and a half decades
Aren't the limit of fame.
Sal fell out of favor long before he was killed.

He came out.
He got older.
He did bad films.
He couldn't find work.
He did cocaine.

A down-and-out actor randomly killed.

I made the film,
It's called *Sal,*
Because I wanted to tell about a life
That had lost its life,
And I wanted to tell it with love.

When My Father Died

I was about to shoot the last scene of the night:
A scene in the Dark Woods,
Opposite a screaming tree
With a mouth and eyes like a jack-o'-lantern.

I was in the chair getting makeup checks,
When my manager called;
My mother was following my father's ambulance,
She had been writing in the back of the house
And she had heard him gasp
In my old room,
His new office,
And that was about all.

Me, a buffoon in cake-thick makeup,
The Wonderful Wizard,
With a set full of people ready for the next shot.

I walked the long halls of the long stage,
And down the Yellow Brick Road,
Where the director, Sam, was waiting.
It was hard to grasp his words,
Like scooping gold fish from a tank
With a broken net
At the kindergarten fair.

Plenty of refrains in my head,
Should I be working?
Should I be racing to the airport?
And they played and played.
I went through the motions of the scene.

We wrapped,
And I got in the car, my driver
Drove me out of the lot
And turned right toward Woodward.

A block away from the studio,
My manager called again.
It was over.

The hanging traffic lights did their work:
Yellow to red as I listened to the cell phone—
My father's spirit was released,
As a green light releases an SUV.

VI.

Film Sonnet 1

The beginning is my favorite part:
All the boys pretend to get romantic
And talk in high voices and blow kisses
At the stuffy teacher's back as he recites
Poetry. The boys flutter and croon.
Then we find out our young hero has
A cheating mother and a weak father,
And he runs away. After all of his
Trouble-making, Antoine Doinel ends
Up at the beach, staring at the ocean
And then staring at us. He's not bad,
He's just lost. The title was always confusing:
400 Blows? Is that porn, S & M?
No, in French it means "to raise hell."

Film Sonnet 2

Marcello is fatigued. A passive-aggressive genius,
A man wrapped in himself: art, mistress, and wife.
He goes to the spa, why? At the spa, people in white
Walk about the plaza, there is a fountain, everyone is rich.
It is something about the water, just the right combination
Of minerals to cure. But no one seems to get healthier,
And no one seems very sick. A conclave to the enclave,
The rich and the sick, Europe's guilty sexual conscience
Spilled out. And this movie is just that, but for one man:
Fellini's getting old, inspiration dries up, but here,
This despair is nice because it is the sorrow of an artist.
An important artist has important despair, and everything
He does can go on the screen: sex, religion, fear.
A confession of pain and proclivities.

Film Sonnet 3

He walks mindlessly, maniacally
Across the desert, like a Sam Shepard man,
A man who has been down to Mexico to die
Of a broken heart but didn't die,
So he comes back to Texas, and then to Los Angeles,
Because all the cowboys retired to the movies.
Now they don't even make Westerns anymore.
Paris, Texas, the name of the place
Where he bought some land, like a slice of Paradise,
But only in his mind. The real place
Is just a deserted plain in the middle of nowhere,
And his wife is working in a peepshow palace,
And you never think, but you should,
He was too old and ugly for her in the first place.

Film Sonnet 4

Wonderful whore, Deneuve, to flow
From the Polanski madness to *Umbrellas* to the housewife
With a penchant for sex. And in that one, I could watch
The john with the swordcane five million times.
His black hair and iron teeth. Good casting, Buñuel:
Pierre Clémenti, later he worked with Bertolucci
On the adaptation of Dostoevsky's *The Double.*
He's also in a little flashback in *The Conformist.*
In *Belle de Jour,* there is a shot of him and Deneuve
That starts on their faces as they make out on the bed,
Then the camera pans over their horizontal legs, to their feet,
At which point Pierre pushes the toe of one wicked black boot against
    the heel
Of the other, and the boot drops to the floor to reveal
A red sock with a hole at the end, his big toe snailing out.

Film Sonnet 5

She begins brokenhearted. She is barred
From her apartment. She has nothing
To eat and walks around Paris one night
With a man she knew before her troubles.
He takes her to a diner and she sleeps with him
For money. First it was the one man and then
Many men. That's called prostitution.
It was easier to fall into everything
Once she had done it the one time.
Sontag called this film "near perfect."
Dreyer's *La Passion de Jeanne d'Arc*
Is stuffed in the middle, whole sections,
A film within a film, to align great suffering
With the suffering of the humble.

Film Sonnet 6

You, Monica Vitti, with your lips, like fruit, how could
That guy in *L'avventura* be blamed for forgetting
The other pouty bitch? If I got a new life I'd pray for
A girl like you. The island where you lose your friend,
Deserted and mysterious. And then after looking
All over Italy for her, you fall for him. And what is
It that compels him, in the aftermath of that party?
In the destroyed room, strewn with plates, silverware,
Food and candlesticks, he with her, on the dislodged
Couch? And what is it that compels you to let it pass,
Just like you let pass the death of a friend?
A mystery. Like in your other Antonioni film, *L'eclisse,*
Which ends with a series of unchanging images:
The building, the sky, a fence, a street.

VII.

Nocturnal

I fight sleep like it's a sickness.
I work up my resistance.
I push it back as far as possible
Every night, like a runner,

Working down his time.
I run through books
And hike through films
And write like a sprinter.

I'm a nocturnal creature,
And I'm here to cheat time.
You can see time and exhaustion
Taking pay from my face—

In fifty years
My sleep will be death,
I'll go like the rest,
But I'll have played

All the games and all the roles.

Brad Renfro

on the fourth anniversary of his death

There is one of two things that happen
When a kid enters the biz.
Either the parents guide that kid
And he becomes a product,

Or he gets no guidance
And he becomes a menace.
Brad Renfro broke out when he was a
Tennessee twelve in *The Client.*

As a newcomer to LA, I remember
Hearing about the wild youngster
High at adult parties,
Making jokes like an adult.

When I worked with him
In *Deuces Wild,* he, the wise age of seventeen,
Had the body of a beat-up,
Balding, beer-bellied adult.

He had played the young version of Brad Pitt
In *Sleepers,* had played opposite Ian McKellen
In *Apt Pupil,* had been a talented little mother,
And then it turned

And he wore out like an engine without oil.
He tried to steal a boat, he got caught in a sweep
In downtown LA that the addicts down there
Talked about for a year.

And when he died, it was a week before Heath,
And because Brad wasn't in *Brokeback,*
And because Brad didn't play the Joker,
The joke was on him; he wasn't even mentioned

At the Oscars, while Heath won the award.
But I remember you, Brad. Not for your warmth,
Or professionalism, or skill,
But because you were someone that was picked up,

Used, fed with drugs, forgotten, and killed.

Directing Herbert White

When Frank wrote "Herbert White" he was a student at Harvard.

•

Frank grew up in Bakersfield, California.

•

Frank had a tough childhood. He wanted to be a filmmaker. He loved film. His mother would drive him to LA to see films.

•

There were only technical film schools in the 1950s, nothing like USC or NYU now, so Frank went to Riverside and studied English, and then went on to Harvard and studied with Robert Lowell.

•

His first book, *Golden State,* was published by Richard Howard. None of the poems had been published in magazines.

•

Golden State, what a fucking title. Frank is the loving son of Lowell and the rebel son of Ginsberg. He is the recondite and the hip.

•

Herbert came out of a cheap, dime-store, medical case study called *21 Abnormal Sex Cases,* cases that included "The Homosexual" and "The Transvestite." Herbert was "The Necrophiliac." In that book he did horrible things, like fuck dogs' stomachs while they were still alive. In Frank's poem Herbert fucks a goat.

•

James got to know Frank when he asked Frank if he could make a movie out of his poem. Frank told James he loved him in *Pineapple Express*.

•

They spent eight hours together the first time they met. They just talked and talked at the restaurant, Frank's regular place in Cambridge, Mass., where he eats every Friday with his buddy Louise Glück. James and Frank stayed after everyone left, oblivious that the restaurant had left a waiter behind to lock the door after them.

•

James knew after hearing the poem read in a class at Warren Wilson that it was something he wanted to adapt into film. These impulses are visceral. It wasn't just because it was about a killer, it was because the killer had been fused with something else. Frank was playing with both sides of the coin again. There are moments in the poem when the killer takes down his mask, and the poet shows through.

•

It wasn't just that Frank had decided to put Herbert's story into lines of verse; Frank had given elements of his own Bakersfield childhood to Herbert. The father, the place, and the desire to make sense of the world were all Frank's.

•

James learned all of this later.

•

Frank also gave Herbert his own young life's isolation and loneliness. This is a guess, but Frank as a young gay man in 1950s Bakersfield must have felt like he had a secret, a secret so dark that he could tell no one. A secret so dark he attempted to become a priest to avoid himself.

●

At the end of the poem it sounds like Herbert is in hell or in jail. He says,

> —Hell came when I saw
> MYSELF . . .
>   and couldn't stand
> what I see . . .

This is a reference to Lowell's "Skunk Hour," "I myself am hell," which references Milton's Satan. There is no way Herbert, without Frank's help, would ever reference Milton.

●

There is a part in the poem,

> Still, I liked to drive past the woods where she lay,
> tell the old lady and the kids I had to take a piss,
> hop out and do it to her . . .
>
> The whole buggy of them waiting for me
>   made me feel good;

He has a family! And they don't know he's a killer! So, he has a deep secret. This was the source of tension that James would use in the film. Herbert has a secret—he's a murderer of women and a fucker of corpses—which he can tell no one.

●

A beautiful thing happened. In the place in Virginia where James was planning to shoot the film, they started tearing down the trees. Huge machines cutting them down and shipping them away. Machines like you've never seen, one with a tractor body and a crane arm at the end of which is a huge claw that clutches whole trees and cuts them with a circular saw in one, two, three seconds, then tosses the trunk like a doll.

●

76

They let the actor playing Herbert, Michael Shannon, get in this machine and drive it for the film.

•

The machine stood in for Herbert's inner life. He cut people down.

•

The man who actually operated the machine for a living was named Gator. He taught Michael Shannon to drive the terrible thing. It was as easy as playing a video game.

•

Once they had the machine as a metaphor they had everything they needed. The machine was the key to the story of Herbert White as told on film.

•

Frank never reads the poem to audiences. The one time he did, back in the 1960s, he warned the audience that it was *not* a confessional poem, because confessional poetry was all the rage in those days. The only way into the hall was a wooden staircase, and after Frank started the reading an elderly woman made her way up the stairs, clop, clop, clop. She came in and listened. She didn't like what she heard. She got up and went back down, right though the reading, clop, clop, clop.

•

The poem is told in the first person, but it isn't Frank speaking. He's wearing a mask. Or two.

•

Frank isn't married. He lives alone among stacks of books and DVDs and CDs. The stacks are so large and numerous they have become his walls.

•

Sometimes, I would like to live in a tight space and be a spy on the world.

Ledger

I've tried to write about you.
I didn't know you.
There was the one time I met you in Teddy's,
The club connected to the Roosevelt Hotel,
The night Prince was playing,

Around the time of all the award shows
When you were nominated for everything
For *Brokeback Mountain*.
And you were with your woman, Michelle;
Two blonds, quiet and stern, mystical.

I wrote a poem about you before,
Back when you died,
But it was coded and unclear
Because I didn't dare write about you openly
Because your death had made you Holy

In Hollywood. You got it all
When you died, you got all
The gold statues because
You were the Joker, with your tongue
Swirling and your death.

There had been a time
When we were up for the same roles,
10 Things I Hate about You
(Based on *The Taming of the Shrew*),
And *The Patriot*—

Funny, you were Australian and so was Mel—
You were the knight in *A Knight's Tale*
Although I'm sure you wished you weren't.
And then something happened,
You played gay and you took off;

You were an artist
For a moment.
Was it too much?
Was it the drugs
That helped you?

The drugs that killed you?
Was it the acting?
Was it all of us,
Outside the screen,
Just watching?

When I Hit Thirty-Four

I looked around for love
And I knew by then
That love wasn't worship,
That love was ease.

Love was the smooth river
Of forgiveness that takes all
Obstacles, pollution and debris
(Love is of man, he sets the rules),

Pushes them downstream
And leaves them in the ocean.
I like the beer bottles that collect
Along the shore, the trash

From diaper boxes and Clorox.
These are rainbow-colored punctuations
Stuck into nature, man-made things
Corroded by my love.

Sometimes things are washed
Clean as when a hurricane
Moves through, sucking up houses
As if they were cardboard.

Love is not of man;
Nature sets the rules.
I've lived a life;
I've learned a few things

And this is a new lesson.
It says, *surrender.*

Telephone

In my parents' old bedroom
With the blue and white wallpaper
Of paisleys and flowers
There was a cream rotary phone.

I'd lie on the bed
That I used to lie on with my dad
As he'd pretend to steal my nose
—It was really just his thumb

Between his fingers—
I'd play with the phone,
Working the circle
Over the numbers

And forcing it back,
Slower than going forward.
My father's middle name
Was Eugene, but when I was young

I'd say "blue jeans." The phone
Was a toy until I had people to call.
One day area codes appeared.
So many numbers to remember.

Now you don't have to remember any.

Love

Love is a woman
Who does many things.
I don't laugh at her
Anymore, she's no fool.

You're the fool
If you think art comes from craft.
Art comes from framing.
Art comes from human imperfection.

Arrogantly, I once wondered
If I would be like Flaubert
Living with a person
Who would never understand my work.

Now I realize that I am understood
Only too well;
I'm a raging Kowalski whose
Temper can be measured by

How little I can give.
How abusive my reticence.
I wish I could turn
And be smacked

With an angel's wallop.
My wandering eye
Is glutted on the world,
But like William Friedkin

Said, after filming fantastic
Landscapes in his failed film
Sorcerer, "Instead of nature,
I should have focused

On the landscape of the human face."

Acknowledgments

Thank you to the editors of the following publications where many of these poems, sometimes in earlier versions, first appeared:

The American Poetry Review: "Los Angeles Proverb" and "Film Sonnet 3"
DIAGRAM: "Directing Herbert White"
The Huffington Post: "31"
The Paris-American: "Hart Crane's Tomb" and "Film Sonnet 6"
Post Road: "Film Sonnet 4" and "Film Sonnet 5"

"Marlon Brando," "Seventh Grade," "Fifth Grade," "Fake," "Nocturnal," "When I Hit Thirty-Four," "Telephone," and "Love" appeared in the chapbook *Strongest of the Litter,* published by Hollyridge Press, 2012.

The ten poems in "The Best of the Smiths" appeared in *113 Crickets,* published by Dymaxicon, summer 2012.

"My Place" and "Second Grade" appeared in *A California Childhood,* published by Insight Editions, 2013.

"River" appeared in *Actors Anonymous,* published by Little A/New Harvest, 2013.

Thank you, Jeff Shotts and everyone at Graywolf, for making this the best book it could be. I have found a home.

Thank you, Richard Abate, for your guidance and belief.

I have been blessed with the best poetry teachers alive: Alan Shapiro, Alan Williamson, Ellen Bryant Voigt, James Longenbach, Rick Barot, Heather McHugh, Tony Hoagland, and Frank Bidart. The Warren Wilson writing program is a little bit of writers' paradise on earth. Thank you to everyone who is a part of it and the three women who made it run while I studied there: Deb Allbery, Amy Grimm, and Alissa Whelan.

Thank you to my family, my friends, fellow writers, fellow filmmakers, Michael Shannon, and everyone else who people these poems. You are in me, and I consist of you.

JAMES FRANCO is an actor, director, writer, and visual artist. He is the author of two works of fiction, *Palo Alto* and *Actors Anonymous,* and a collage of memoir, snapshots, poems, and artwork, *A California Childhood.* His poetry has appeared in a chapbook, *Strongest of the Litter. Directing Herbert White* is Franco's first full-length book of poetry. His writing has also been published in *Esquire,* the *Huffington Post, McSweeney's, n+1, Vanity Fair,* and the *Wall Street Journal.* He has received MFAs in fiction from Brooklyn College and Columbia, an MFA in film from New York University, an MFA in art from Rhode Island School of Design, and an MFA in poetry from Warren Wilson College.

Franco's film appearances include *Milk, Pineapple Express,* and *127 Hours,* which earned him an Academy Award nomination. He portrayed Allen Ginsberg in the film *Howl,* and Hart Crane in *The Broken Tower,* a film Franco adapted and directed. He has also adapted many poems into films that he has directed, including short films based on "Herbert White" by Frank Bidart, the collection *Black Dog, Red Dog* by Stephen Dobyns, "The Clerk's Tale" by Spencer Reece, and the collection *Tar* by C. K. Williams. Franco has also adapted to film the novels *As I Lay Dying* by William Faulkner and *Child of God* by Cormac McCarthy.

He lives in New York and Los Angeles.

The text of *Directing Herbert White* is set in Dante—a font designed by Italian printer, book designer, and typeface artist Giovanni Mardersteig. Book design by Rachel Holscher. Composition by BookMobile Design & Digital Publisher Services, Minneapolis, Minnesota. Manufactured by Versa Press on acid-free, 30 percent postconsumer wastepaper.